NEW HORIZONS

OXFORD

Secular

SSATB and piano or string orchestra

— CECILIA McDOWALL —

Shipping Forecast

First performed on 18 June 2011 in Portsmouth Cathedral, as part of the Portsmouth Festivities, by the Portsmouth Festival Choir, conducted by Andrew Cleary.

An accompaniment for string orchestra is also available on rental from the publisher's Hire Library or appropriate agent.

1. Shipping Forecast, Donegal

They have shared still late October,
but salt stones and a broken tree,
the peeled paint on the lifeboat house
chime with places where the glass falls,
prime sources encountering night's bald predictions.

Everywhere winter edges in,
and now the time is ten to six…

lightness and weight, air's potentials
pressed into words, implication;
here – on all coasts – listening grows passionately tense.

Fair Isle, Faeroes, South East Iceland,
North Utsire, South Utsire,
Fisher, German Bight, Tyne, Dogger…
This pattern of names on the sea –
weather's unlistening geography – paves water.
Beyond the music, the singing
of sounds – this minimal chanting,
this ritual pared to the bone
becomes the cold poetry of information.

The litany edges closer –

Lundy, Fastnet and Irish Sea…
Routine enough, all just routine.
Always his eyes guessing beyond
the headland, she perhaps sleeping, no words spoken.

He stretches forward to grasp it,
claims his radio place – *and now*
the weather reports from coastal stations
and then: *Malin Head* – such routine
that she barely glances up, but hears *now falling.*

Seán Street

2. Psalm 107 | 23-26:28-29

They that go down to the sea in ships

They that go down to the sea in ships: and occupy their business in great waters; These men see the works of the Lord: and his wonders in the deep. For at his word the stormy wind ariseth: which lifteth up the waves thereof. They are carried up to the heaven, and down again to the deep: their soul melteth away because of the trouble. So when they cry unto the Lord in their trouble: he delivereth them out of their distress. For he maketh the storm to cease: so that the waves thereof are still.

The Book of Common Prayer 1662

3. Naming (The Broadcast)

Belle Isle, Come-by-Chance, Cabot Strait.
Every name's a story, but weathers change,
tides overwrite and meanings ebb.
Happy Adventure, Great Paradise, Fortune Head.
Every name's a story until new stories come
where men after men die fighting the sea for a harbour.
Funk Island, Mistaken Point, Snakes Bight,
Savage Cove, Wreck Cove, Deadman's Bay.
Every name's a story.
Every day, new stories come.

Seán Street

Commissioned by the Portsmouth Festival Choir in celebration of its 40th Anniversary, conductor Andrew Cleary

Shipping Forecast

Seán Street | Shipping Forecast

I

Donegal

CECILIA McDOWALL

© Oxford University Press 2011
Cecilia McDowall has asserted her right under the Copyright, Designs and Patents Act, 1988, to be identified as Composer of this work.
OXFORD UNIVERSITY PRESS, GREAT CLARENDON STREET, OXFORD OX2 6DP.
Photocopying this copyright material is ILLEGAL

13
p
— the peeled paint on the life - boat house
mf sim.
chime, chime,
p
— the peeled paint on the life - boat house
mf sim.
chime, chime,
p
— the peeled paint on the life - boat house
mf sim.
chime, chime,
mp
tree,
mf leggiero
chime with
mp
tree,
mf leggiero
chime with
mf
19
mf
chime with pla - ces where the glass falls,
chime, chime, chime, chime, chime, glass falls, falls, falls,
chime, chime, chime, chime, chime, glass falls, falls,
pla - ces where the glass, glass falls, falls,
pla - ces where the glass, glass falls, falls,

24
mp dolce
cresc.
prime sour - ces
en - coun - ter - ing night's bald pre - dic - tions.
prime,
en - coun - ter - ing, bald pre - dic - tions.
prime,
en - coun - ter - ing, bald pre - dic - tions.
prime sour - ces,
prime sour - ces,
mp
prime,
en -
mf
30
f
Ev - 'ry - where, ev - 'ry, ev - 'ry - where, win - ter,
Ev - 'ry - where, ev - 'ry, ev - 'ry - where, win - ter,
Ev - 'ry - where, ev - 'ry, ev - 'ry - where, win - ter,
Ev - 'ry - where, ev - 'ry, ev - 'ry - where, win - ter,
coun - ter - ring. Ev - 'ry, ev - 'ry, ev - 'ry, win - ter,

35

mf legato e cresc. — *sub.* **p** — **ritardando** — **pp**

win - ter ed - ges, ed - ges in,

mf legato e cresc. — *sub.* **p** — **pp**

win - ter ed - ges, ed - ges in,

mf legato e cresc. — *sub.* **p** — **pp**

win - ter ed - ges, ed - ges in,

mf legato e cresc. — *sub.* **p** — **pp**

win - ter ed - ges, ed - ges in,

mf legato e cresc. — ***SOLO** — **f** *spoken naturally* — **BASSES tutti**

win - ter ed - ges, ed - ges, *and now the time is ten to six*

ritardando

mf legato e cresc. — *sub.* **p**

SOPRANOS 1 & 2

a tempo

40

S.1 & 2 — **pp** *dolciss.* — **p** — *cresc.* — **poco rit.**

light-ness and weight, air, air's po - ten - tials pressed in - to

A. — **pp** *dolciss.* — *cresc.*

light-ness and weight, air, air's po - ten - tials pressed in - to

T. — **pp** *dolciss.* — *cresc.*

im - pli - ca - tion; pressed, pressed, pressed in - to

B. — **pp** *dolciss.* — *cresc.*

im - pli - ca - tion, im - pli - ca - tion; pressed, pressed

a tempo — **poco rit.**

p *sonorous*

8vb

***Solo:** either a male soloist or a bass from the chorus. To be spoken freely, announced in the manner of the BBC Shipping Forecast.

Meno mosso ♩ = *c.*69

45

S.1: *mf* words, *p cresc. poco a poco* here, on all

S.2: *mf* words, *p cresc. poco a poco* on all,

A.: *mf* words, *p cresc. poco a poco* on all

T.: *mf* words, *p* list'n-

B.: *mf* in - to words,

Meno mosso ♩ = *c.*69

Piano: *mf* *legato* *mp* *molto Ped.* 8vb

48

S.1: coasts, all, *f* all,

S.2: on all, on all, *f* on all,

A.: coasts, on all coasts, on all *f* coasts, on all

T.: *cresc. poco a poco* - - ing grows, grows, *f* pas -

B.: *p cresc. poco a poco* list'n - ing grows, grows, *f* pas -

Piano: *cresc. poco a poco* *f*

51
dim.
all coasts, all coasts, all coasts,
on all, all coasts, all coasts,
coasts, on all coasts, on all coasts, on all coasts
sion - ate - ly tense, tense, grows tense.
sion - ate - ly tense, grows tense.
dim.
54
all.
all.
all.
p dolce

57
mp dolce
This pat - tern of names
SOLO (spoken)
f
Fair Isle, Fae - roes, South East Ice - land
3
mp
60
mf
Ah
mf
Ah
mf
on the
North Ut-sire, South Ut-sire, Fish-er, Ger-man Bight, Tyne, Dog-ger,
mf

63
f
on
the
sea,
f
on
the
sea,
sea,
mf
sea,
BASSES tutti
f
66
mf
weath-er's un - list'n - ing geo-gra - phy, paves wa - - - - ter.
3
mf
3
3

69
Tempo primo ♩ = c.92
p
cresc.
Be - yond the mu - sic, the sing - ing of sounds,
Be - yond, the sing - ing of
Be - yond, the sing - ing of
Be - yond, sounds,
sounds,
74
f
mf
of sounds, chant - ing, chant - ing,
sounds, of sounds, chant - ing, chant - ing,
sounds, of sounds, chant - ing, chant - ing,
of sounds, chant - ing, chant - ing,
this mi - ni - mal chant - ing, chant - ing,

79
legato e cresc.
sub.p
chant - ing, chant- ing, this rit - ual pared to the bone.
chant - ing, chant- ing, this rit - ual pared to the bone.
chant - ing, chant- ing, this rit - ual pared to the bone.
chant - ing, chant- ing, this rit - ual pared to the bone.
SOLO (spoken) f
chant - ing, chant- ing, this rit - ual pared, pared, be-comes the cold po-e-try of
84
ritardando
a tempo
pp
p dolce
The lit - a - ny edges clos - er,
The lit - a - ny ed - ges clos - er,
The lit - a - ny ed - ges clos - er,
pp dolciss.
Lit - a - ny ed - ges,
BASSES tutti
in - for-ma-tion. Lit - a - ny ed - ges clos - er,
8vb

SOPRANOS 1 & 2
89
p
pp
mp legato
Rou - tine e - nough all just rou - tine.
Al -
A.
Rou - tine e - nough, all just rou - tine.
Al -
T.
ed - ges clos - er.
B.
SOLO (spoken)
f
BASSES tutti
clos - er,
Lun-dy, Fast-net and I - rish Sea,
(8)
94
ways his eyes guess-ing be - yond the head-land, no words spo - ken.
ways his eyes guess-ing be - yond the head-land, no words spo - ken.
sleep - ing, she per - haps sleep-ing, sleep - ing.
sleep-ing, she per-haps sleep - ing.
p espress. e legato
R.H.

*Pauses if required for soloist to complete spoken phrases.

112
mf
sim.
-tine that she bare-ly glan - ces up, fall - ing, fall - ing,
mf
sim.
-tine that she bare-ly glan - ces up, fall - ing, fall - ing,
mf
sim.
-tine that she bare-ly glan - ces up, fall - ing, fall - ing,
mp
mf leggiero
then, fall, fall,
mp
mf leggiero
then, fall, fall,
mf
117
mf
ritardando
pp
lunga
fall - - - - ing, but hears now fall - - ing.
dim.
pp
lunga
fall-ing, fall-ing, fall-ing, fall - ing, fall - ing, fall - ing, fall - - ing.
dim.
pp
lunga
fall-ing, fall-ing, fall-ing, fall - ing, fall - ing, fall - ing, fall - - ing.
dim.
lunga
fall - ing, fall - ing, fall - ing.
dim.
Solo (spoken) mf
lunga
fall - ing, fall - ing, fall - ing. now fall - ing.
ritardando
lunga
mp
lunga

II
They that go down to the sea in ships

Psalm 107: 23–6, 28–9

19
S.
A.
T.
B.
mf
in the deep.
mf
and his won - ders in the deep, deep.
25
mf cresc.
For at his word the stor - - - - my wind a-
f
mf
f

30
mp cresc.
which lift - eth up.
mp cresc.
which lift - eth up the waves there - of.
- ris - eth:
mf
36
mf cresc.
They are car-ried up to hea ven,
f
mf cresc.
They are car - ried up to hea - ven,
f
and down a-
f
and down, down
f
mf
f

41
f
hea - ven,
their
f
hea - ven,
their
-gain to the deep:
a-gain to the deep, deep:
mf
Ped. ad lib.
47
espress.
mf dim. poco a poco
soul melt - eth, their soul melt - eth,
espress.
mf dim. poco a poco
soul melt - eth a - way, be - cause of the trou - ble,
f espress.
mf dim. poco a poco
their soul melt - eth, their soul melt -
f espress.
mf dim. poco a poco
their soul melt - eth a - way, be - cause of the
f
mf dim. poco a poco

53
melt - - eth.
melt - eth.
-eth, melt - - eth.
trou - ble, melt - - eth.
mp
6
59
mf
So when they cry un - to the Lord in their trou - ble: he de - liv - - er -
So when they cry un - to the Lord in their trou - ble: he de - liv - er-eth them out of their dis -
So when they cry un - to the Lord in their trou - ble: he de - liv - - - er -
So when they cry un - to the Lord in their trou - ble: he de - liv - er-eth them out of their dis -
f

65
mp
- eth. For, for he
mp
- tress. For he
mp
- eth. For,
mp
- tress. For he
mp
mp
mf
p sempre dolce
71
mak - eth the storm to cease, to cease:
mak - - eth the storm, the storm to cease, to
for he mak - eth the storm to cease, to
mak - - eth the storm, the storm to cease,

76
mp
so that the waves there - of are
cease: so that the waves there - of are
cease: so that the waves there - of
to cease: so that the waves there - of
83
p dolce (stagger breathing)
still, so that
p dolce
still, so that the waves there
are still.
are still, still.
p
mp
(p sempre dolce)

*In *The Fisheries Broadcast*, Newfoundland, *Cabot* is prounounced with a voiced T

* *stacc. sim.* - to be played *mezzo staccato,* not dry.

11

S. *f* *mf* Ev - - - 'ry name's a sto - ry, *mf* ev -

A. *f* *mf* Ev - - - 'ry name's a sto - ry, *mf* ev -

T. *mf* Ev - - - 'ry name's a sto - ry, *mf* ev -

B. *mf* Ev - - - 'ry name's a sto - ry, *mf* ev -

L.H.

f *legato* *mf*

16

S. - 'ry, *mf* ev - 'ry name's a sto - ry,

A. - 'ry, *mf* ev - 'ry name's a sto - ry,

T. - 'ry, *mf* ev - 'ry name's a sto - ry,

B. - 'ry, *mf* ev - 'ry name's a sto - ry,

21

mp dolce — *mp cresc.*

but weath-ers change, — but weath - ers,

mp dolce — *mp cresc.*

but weath-ers change, — but weath - ers change,

mp dolce — *mp cresc.*

but weath - ers change, — but weath - ers,

mp dolce — *mp cresc.*

but weath-ers change, — but weath - ers,

mp *cantabile*

26

mf *f*

weath - ers change, change,

mf *f*

weath - ers change, change,

mf *f*

weath - ers change, change,

mf *f*

weath - ers change, change,

mf *f*

31
mp
tides
mp
o - - - ver - - - -
mp
tides o - ver -
mp espress.
36
mp
o - - - ver - write
mf cresc.
and mean - ings ebb,
o - - ver - - write
mf cresc.
and mean - ings
- write,
mf cresc.
mean - - ings ebb,
- write
and mean - ings
mf cresc.
ebb,
and mean - ings
mf cresc.

41
f
— ebb, ebb.
ebb, ebb, ebb.
mean - ings ebb, ebb.
ebb, ebb, ebb.
46
mf sempre leggiero e ritmico
For - - tune
Hap-py Ad-ven - ture, Great Pa-ra - dise, For - tune
Hap-py Ad - ven-ture, Great Pa - ra - dise, Hap-py Ad-ven - ture, Great Pa-ra-dise, Great
mf sempre leggiero e ritimco
Hap-py Ad - ven-ture, Great Pa-ra - dise, Great, Hap-py Ad-ven - ture, Great
mf
Ped.

51
mp cresc.
— Head, Hap - py Ad - ven - ture, Great_ Pa - ra - dise, Hap - py Ad - ven -
Head, Hap - py Ad - ven - ture Great_ Pa - ra - dise, Hap - py Ad - ven - ture Great
— Pa - ra - dise, Great_ Pa - ra - dise,_ Great_ Pa - ra - dise, Great_ Pa - ra - dise,_ Great_
— Pa - ra - dise, Great_ Pa - ra - dise,_ Great_ Pa - ra - dise,_ Great_ Pa - ra - dise,_ Great_
Ped.
55
f
mf
- ture, Great_ Pa - ra - dise. Ev - - 'ry name's a sto - ry, ev -
— Pa - ra - dise, dise,_ Ev - - 'ry name's a sto - ry, ev -
— Pa - ra - dise,_ dise,_ Ev - - 'ry name's a sto - ry, ev -
— Pa - ra dise,_ dise,_ Ev - - 'ry name's a sto - ry, ev -
Ped. sim.

60
mf
- 'ry, ev - - - 'ry name's a sto - ry, un -
- 'ry, ev - - - 'ry name's a sto - ry, sto -
- 'ry, ev - - - 'ry name's a sto - ry, sto -
- 'ry, ev - - - 'ry name's a sto - ry, sto -
65
f
-til new sto - ries come
- ries come
- ries come men
- ries come where men
mp
mp espress.

71
mp cresc. poco a poco
men die fight - ing the
mp cresc. poco a poco
men aft - er men die
cresc. poco a poco
die, men die
cresc. poco a poco
aft - er men die fight - ing the sea
mf cresc.
76
f
sea for a har - bour.
f
fight - ing.
f
fight - ing.
f
for a har - bour.
f

81

mf

Wreck,

mf leggiero

Snakes Bight, Sa - vage Cove, Wreck,

mf leggiero e ritmico

Funk Is - land, Mis - ta - ken Point, Snakes Bight, Sa - vage Cove, Wreck

mf leggiero e ritmico

Funk Is - land, Mis - ta - ken Point, Snakes Bight,

mf

Ped.

85

Wreck Cove,

Wreck Cove,

Cove, Wreck Cove, Snakes Bight, Sa - vage Cove, Wreck

Funk Is - land, Mis - ta - ken Point, Snakes Bight, Sa - vage Cove,

Ped.

89
f
This pat - tern of names
f
This pat - tern of names
Cove, Wreck Cove, Snakes Bight, Sa - vage Cove, Wreck
Funk Is - land, Mis - ta - ken Point, Snakes Bight, Sa - vage Cove,
Ped.
93
on
f
on
Cove, Wreck Cove, Snakes Bight, Sa - vage Cove, Wreck
Funk Is - land, Mis - ta - ken Point Snakes Bight, Sa - vage Cove,
Ped.

97
mp leggiero
the sea.
Hap - py Ad - ven -
the sea.
Hap - py Ad - ven - ture, Great
mp
Cove, Wreck Cove, Snakes Bight, Dead - man's Bay, Dead-
Funk Is - land, Mis - ta - ken Point, Snakes Bight, Dead - man's Bay, Dead-
mp
Ped.
101
mf
- ture, Great Pa-ra - dise, Hap-py Ad-ven - ture, Great Pa-ra - dise.
Ev
Pa-ra-dise, Hap - py Ad-ven-ture, Great Pa-ra-dise, dise.
Ev
- man's Bay, Dead - man's Bay, Dead - man's Bay, Bay.
Ev
- man's Bay, Dead - man's Bay, Dead - man's Bay, Bay.
Ev
f
mf
Ped.

106
- 'ry name's a sto - ry, ev - - - 'ry, ev - - - - 'ry name's a
Ped. sim.
111
mf
f
sto - - ry, new sto - ries come, ev - 'ry, ev - 'ry day.
Ped.

NEW HORIZONS

NEW HORIZONS showcases the wealth of exciting, innovative, and occasionally challenging choral music being written today. It encompasses the whole gamut of small-scale choral genres, both secular and sacred, and includes pieces for upper-voice and mixed choirs. With titles by some of the most accomplished choral composers active in Great Britain and abroad, the series introduces new repertoire and fresh talent to a broad spectrum of choirs.

Cecilia McDowall

Photo: Christie Dickason

Born in 1951 and educated at Edinburgh and London Universities, Cecilia McDowall has been described by the International Record Review as having a 'communicative gift that is very rare in modern music'. An award-winning composer, McDowall is often inspired by extra-musical influences, and her choral writing combines rhythmic vitality with expressive lyricism. Her music has been commissioned, performed, and recorded by leading choirs, among them Phoenix Chorale and the Choir of New College, Oxford, and is regularly programmed at prestigious festivals in Britain and abroad.

OXFORD
UNIVERSITY PRESS

www.oup.com

ISBN 978-0-19-337972-5

9 780193 379725